The Law Commission

(LAW COM No 354)

TWELFTH PROGRAMME OF LAW REFORM

Prese ... of the Law Comm

Order ... rinted on 21 Jul

HC 364

The original HM Government publication is available at
www.gov.uk/government/publications

This edition printed and published in the UK by The Stationery Office Limited

Printed on paper containing 75% recycled fibre content minimum.

THE LAW COMMISSION

The Law Commission was set up by the Law Commissions Act 1965 for the purpose of promoting the reform of the law.

The Law Commissioners are:

The Right Honourable Lord Justice Lloyd Jones, *Chairman*
Professor Elizabeth Cooke
Mr David Hertzell
Professor David Ormerod QC
Mr Nicholas Paines QC

The Chief Executive of the Law Commission is Mrs Elaine Lorimer.

The Law Commission is located at 1st Floor, Tower, 52 Queen Anne's Gate, London, SW1H 9AG.

The terms of this report were agreed on 8 July 2014.

The text of this document is available on the Law Commission's website at www.lawcom.gov.uk.

LAW COMMISSION

TWELFTH PROGRAMME OF LAW REFORM

CONTENTS

LAW COMMISSION

TWELFTH PROGRAMME OF LAW REFORM

To the Right Honourable Chris Grayling MP, Lord Chancellor and Secretary of State for Justice

PART 1
INTRODUCTION

BACKGROUND

1.1 The Law Commission was established by the Law Commissions Act 1965 for the purpose of promoting the reform of the law. The Law Commission is required to receive and consider proposals for law reform and to prepare and submit to the Lord Chancellor, from time to time, programmes for the examination of different branches of the law with a view to reform.[1]

1.2 This Twelfth Programme of Law Reform will run from July 2014.

CONSULTATION

1.3 The Law Commission consults widely when drawing up programmes of law reform, in order to ensure that our work is as relevant and informed as possible. Consultation for the Twelfth Programme was launched on 2 July 2013 with an event at the Royal Institution of Great Britain. This was attended by members of the senior judiciary and leading legal practitioners, as well as representatives from the private, public and third sectors and academia. The consultation then ran until 31 October.

1.4 During this period, the Chairman, Commissioners and Chief Executive met Supreme Court judges and held a seminar at the Royal Courts of Justice for Court of Appeal and High Court judges. The Commission also held a consultation event in the House of Lords for MPs and peers, and staged a week-long exhibition in the Houses of Parliament to advertise the consultation.

1.5 Meetings were held with the Lord Chancellor and Secretary of State for Justice; the Attorney General; the Secretary of State for Business, Innovation and Skills; the Minister of State for Civil Justice and Legal Policy; the Minister of State for Policing, Criminal Justice and Victims; the Minister for Prisons and Rehabilitation; and the Minister for the Cabinet Office. The Chief Executive also met legal and policy directors across Whitehall and the Chief Executives of the Law Commissions in Scotland and Northern Ireland.

1 Law Commissions Act 1965, s 3(1)(a) and (b)

1.6 The Chairman met the Bar Council's Law Reform Committee and the Law Society. Information on the consultation was distributed to professional associations, legal academic groups, public sector organisations, and membership and umbrella organisations in the private and third sectors. Teams also notified their existing contacts of the opportunity to submit proposals. The Commission publicised the details more widely through articles in the legal and third sector media, as well as via its website and Twitter account. In addition, a number of events were held specifically to promote the consultation in Wales. More details on these can be found below.

1.7 Questionnaires were made available to consultees both electronically and in hard copy, and an online response facility was set up. Around 20% of consultees used this facility. In total, the Commission received over 250 proposals from 180 consultees. Although a handful of projects were suggested multiple times, the vast majority of proposals were submitted by only one or two consultees.

1.8 For the first time, the Commission also published its own suggestions for areas of the law that might benefit from reform. These were generated following discussions both internally and with stakeholders, and consultees were invited to comment on them. Over 80 consultees did so, and four of these suggested projects have been included in the final programme. A full list of the Commission's suggestions can be found in Appendix A.

1.9 The Law Commission would like to thank everyone who contributed to the Twelfth Programme consultation. We were delighted at the enthusiastic response and the wide variety of ideas that were generated by consultees. We believe that this has allowed us to develop a diverse and valuable programme of law reform.

WALES

1.10 The Law Commission covers the jurisdiction of England and Wales. Recently, the National Assembly for Wales gained direct primary legislative powers in devolved areas of the law. The Commission is committed to meeting the law reform needs of both England and Wales in this new constitutional context. We have already published our first bilingual report,[2] and the Welsh Assembly has recently passed its first Act to implement a Law Commission report.[3]

1.11 The Law Commission is currently taking steps to ensure that the appropriate machinery is in place for the future delivery of effective law reform in Wales. The Commission established a Welsh Advisory Committee in 2013 to assist in identifying the law reform needs of Wales in both devolved and non-devolved areas of the law. The Wales Bill currently before Parliament contains a provision to amend the Law Commissions Act 1965 which will, amongst other things, enable Welsh Ministers to refer projects directly to the Commission.

[2] Renting Homes in Wales, Rhentu Cartrefi yng Nghymru (2013) Law Com No 337

[3] Social Services and Well-being (Wales) Act 2014

1.12 The Law Commission held a Twelfth Programme consultation event at the Wales Governance Centre, Cardiff, in October 2013. The keynote address was given by Theodore Huckle QC, Counsel General to the Welsh Government. This event was attended by representatives of the legal profession, academia, and the private, public and third sectors in Wales. The Commission also attended the Legal Wales Conference 2013, where the Chairman spoke about the Twelfth Programme and discussed proposals for potential projects.

1.13 We received numerous consultation responses from Welsh consultees, including proposals for projects in devolved areas of the law. The Commission also suggested one project relating exclusively to Wales. The Welsh Advisory Committee has considered the proposals received at two stages and provided valuable input, both in relation to the Wales-only projects and to the impact in Wales of other suggested projects. The final programme contains an advisory project and a full law reform project relating to Wales. A further project, relating to environmental law in Wales, did not receive the Lord Chancellor's approval as required by section 3(1)(c) of the Law Commissions Act 1965 and has therefore not been included in the programme.

THE LAW COMMISSION'S PROJECT SELECTION CRITERIA

1.14 This is the second programme of law reform to be developed under the terms of the Protocol between the Lord Chancellor and the Law Commission, which was given statutory backing by the Law Commission Act 2009.[4] The Protocol explains how Government and the Law Commission work together, and establishes the procedure for creating a programme of law reform.

1.15 When considering whether to include a project in the Twelfth Programme, the Law Commission assessed each proposal against the following selection criteria:

(1) Importance: the extent to which the law is unsatisfactory (for example, unfair, unduly complex, inaccessible or outdated), and the potential benefits of reform.

(2) Suitability: whether the independent, non-political Commission is the most suitable body to conduct the project.

(3) Resources: whether the necessary resources, including project-specific funding, are available to enable the project to be carried out effectively.

1.16 The Protocol also required consideration of:

(1) whether there is a Scottish or Northern Irish dimension to the project that needs the involvement of the Scottish and/or Northern Ireland Law Commissions;

(2) whether there is a Welsh dimension that needs the involvement of the Welsh Government; and

[4] Protocol between the Lord Chancellor (on behalf of the Government) and the Law Commission (2010) Law Com No 321, HC 499

(3) the degree of departmental support for the project. Under the terms of the Protocol, the Lord Chancellor will expect the relevant department to indicate a serious intention to take forward law reform in the area before approving the inclusion of a project in the programme.

CONFIRMED PROJECTS FOR THE TWELFTH PROGRAMME

1.17 Having applied the criteria set out above, Commissioners have selected the following projects for the Twelfth Programme of Law Reform.

Name of project	Policy responsibility
Bills of sale	Department for Business, Innovation and Skills
Firearms: scoping project	Home Office
The form and accessibility of the law applicable in Wales: advisory project	Welsh Government/Wales Office/Ministry of Justice
Land registration	Department for Business, Innovation and Skills/Land Registry
Mental capacity and detention	Department of Health
Planning and development control in Wales	Welsh Government
Protecting consumer prepayments on retailer insolvency	Department for Business, Innovation and Skills
Sentencing procedure	Ministry of Justice
Wills	Ministry of Justice

1.18 Each of these projects is explained in more detail in Part 2.

FURTHER PROJECTS

1.19 The Law Commission also undertakes advisory work for Government and projects referred directly by Ministers.[5] This may form part of our work during the course of the Twelfth Programme. In Part 3, we summarise a number of other proposals that we have not been able to take forward in the Twelfth Programme, but which we may be able to accept as references from Ministers if resources become available.

1.20 In addition, the Commission will continue its work on projects from previous programmes, as well as statute law repeals and consolidation. Further details on the wider work of the Commission can be found on our website.

5 Law Commissions Act 1965, s 3(1)(a) and (e)

WORKING WITH OTHER LAW COMMISSIONS

1.21 The Law Commission's role covers the law of England and Wales, but not the law of Scotland or the law of Northern Ireland. We undertake joint projects with the Scottish and/or Northern Ireland Law Commissions where the existing law operates across multiple jurisdictions. Two such joint projects are currently ongoing. However, no new joint projects have been included in the Twelfth Programme.

PART 2
TWELFTH PROGRAMME PROJECTS

INTRODUCTION

2.1 In this Part we set out the new projects we will be undertaking. Some of these projects are already well defined, while the parameters of others will be clarified only after a scoping study.

BILLS OF SALE

Summer 2014 – summer 2016

2.2 A bill of sale is a way in which persons may use their existing goods as security for a loan. A contemporary example is the "logbook loan", often used because the borrower is unable to access credit from mainstream lenders. The use of bills of sale has grown dramatically recently, from 2,840 in 2001 to 38,000 by 2008, a level which appears to have been sustained in the past five years. In the future, their use may increase further.

2.3 The law in this area, set out in the Bills of Sale Acts 1878 and 1882, is complex, arcane and out-dated. The archaic language of the governing Acts is all but impenetrable, and consumers and businesses borrowing in this way rarely understand the effects of their transactions. The Acts impose unnecessary costs on businesses, while depriving consumers of the standard protections for other forms of credit. A default on the loan can result in the property being seized, in many cases without any notice.

2.4 The consequences of not following the exacting formality requirements are also severe: an error will make the bill void. Every bill must be registered, but the registration scheme is difficult to use and search, and has not made use of technological advances. The Citizens Advice Bureau has argued that "the present regulatory and legislative framework governing logbook lending is untenable", and that the introduction of a voluntary code of practice has not diminished the need for legal reform.

2.5 This project will review the existing legislation and the registration regime for bills of sale, and make recommendations for the modernisation and simplification of the law. The project will also consider the growing use of bills of sale in the consumer credit market, and particularly the question of whether there is adequate protection for borrowers.

FIREARMS: SCOPING PROJECT

Spring 2015 – spring 2016

2.6 Criminal offences relating to firearms are inadequate. This is causing real difficulties for investigating authorities and prosecutors. In part, this is because the way weapons were categorised in legislation and understood in society almost half a century ago no longer reflects the present reality.

2.7 Furthermore, some important statutory terms, such as "antique", remain undefined. Thus, when presented with a weapon of a certain age, it can be challenging for investigators to determine whether it falls foul of an offence-creating provision. A mistake at this stage can have ramifications for the success of a prosecution. There are many examples in the decided cases where defendants have availed themselves of a technical defence, successfully arguing that the weapon they undoubtedly had in their possession was wrongly described by the prosecution. As a result, they have been prosecuted under the wrong provision of the wrong statute and are acquitted.

2.8 Public confidence in the criminal justice system is severely dented when defendants walk free because the statutes designed to criminalise their behaviour are not fit for use in the modern age. This scoping exercise will survey the current landscape, identify the problems with the law and propose a range of reform possibilities. It will consider the enactment of a single firearms statute bringing together the offence-creating provisions currently embedded in a number of Acts, along with more limited options, perhaps aimed at particular problem areas in the current law. On the basis of our analysis, the Home Office and the Commission will then decide whether to take the project further.

THE FORM AND ACCESSIBILITY OF THE LAW APPLICABLE IN WALES: ADVISORY PROJECT

Summer 2014 – late 2015

2.9 Problems with the form and accessibility of the law relating to Wales have been apparent for some time, and are becoming more serious. The particular history of devolution in Wales has resulted in a situation in which it is difficult for both professionals and the public to access the law relating to Wales.

2.10 Under the Government of Wales Act 1998, executive powers were transferred by numerous transfer of functions orders to the National Assembly for Wales. During this phase of devolution, other powers were transferred to the Welsh Assembly by statute. In 2007, these functions were transferred to Welsh Ministers. The result is that it can be very difficult to ascertain who exercises executive powers. A power which, on the face of a statute, appears to be exercised by the Secretary of State may in fact have been transferred to Welsh Ministers. However, this will not be apparent without in-depth research.

2.11 Furthermore, before 2006, primary legislation could generally only be amended by Westminster. On a number of occasions, amendments were made at the behest of the Welsh Government. Following the introduction of the system in Part 3 of the Government of Wales Act 2006, legislative powers could be transferred to the Welsh Assembly by statute or by Legislative Consent Order. In 2011, Part 4 of the 2006 Act came into force, giving the Welsh Assembly broader powers to make laws in devolved areas. However, Welsh legislation is still based on pre-devolution statutes. These may have been subsequently amended by both Parliament and the Welsh Assembly, so that they now contain some provisions that cover England and Wales, some that relate to England, and some that are specific to Wales only.

2.12 This project will consider ways in which the earlier legislation could be simplified and made more accessible, and how future legislation could reduce, rather than multiply, the problems. The project will be purely advisory, and our final report will not contain a draft Bill.

LAND REGISTRATION

Autumn 2014 – autumn 2017

2.13 The Land Registration Act 2002 established a regime for the registration of title to freehold and some leasehold land, and interests affecting such land. The 2002 Act was implemented following a joint project between the Law Commission and Land Registry.

2.14 The land registration regime is of enormous and growing importance. Over 80% of the land in England and Wales is registered, with Land Registry maintaining more than 23 million titles. Dealings and disputes that engage the land registration regime can be complex and require expert advice. Uncertainty in the regime makes advising clients difficult, incentivises litigation, and increases costs for landowners.

2.15 This project will comprise a wide-ranging review of the 2002 Act, with a view to amendment where elements of the Act could be improved in light of experience with its operation. There is evidence that, in some areas, revision or clarification is needed. The Twelfth Programme consultation revealed a range of often highly technical issues that have important commercial implications for Land Registry and its stakeholders, including mortgage providers.

2.16 In particular, this project will examine the extent of Land Registry's guarantee of title, rectification and alteration of the register, and the impact of fraud. The project will also re-examine the legal framework for electronic conveyancing. We will consider how technology might be harnessed to reduce the time and resources required to process applications, while maintaining the reliability of the register and public confidence in it.

MENTAL CAPACITY AND DETENTION

Summer 2014 – summer 2017

2.17 Arrangements made for treating persons who lack capacity to consent to their treatment can amount to deprivations of liberty that contravene their human rights. In 2007, the deprivation of liberty safeguards (DOLS) were introduced into the Mental Capacity Act 2005 to ensure that such deprivations of liberty are properly regulated in accordance with human rights legislation. This means that people who lack capacity to consent to their treatment can be deprived of their liberty in a hospital or care home if it is considered necessary in their best interests. The hospital or care home as the "managing authority" must apply to its local council (the "supervisory body") for authorisation of a deprivation of liberty. The supervisory body will then assess whether the deprivation is legal.

2.18 DOLS have been subject to considerable criticism ever since their introduction. In March 2014, a House of Lords select committee concluded that DOLS were not "fit for purpose" and proposed their replacement. The committee recommended that the replacement legislation extend to those living in supported living arrangements, not just hospitals and care homes. The Department of Health has accepted that there are difficulties with DOLS and has announced various measures to improve their operation.

2.19 This project will consider a new legal framework to allow for the authorisation of best interests deprivations of liberty in supported living and other community care settings, in accordance with the select committee's recommendations. We will also consider changes that will have to be made to DOLS to take account of the outcome of our work.

PLANNING AND DEVELOPMENT CONTROL IN WALES

Summer 2014 – summer 2017

2.20 Planning law in both England and Wales is over-complicated and difficult to understand. The statutory provisions have not been consolidated since the Town and Country Planning Act 1990, and there has been piecemeal legislative development ever since. The position is even more complex in Wales. Some, but not all, of the recent English legislation is applicable to Wales, and there are some provisions that are specific to Wales only. Some statutory provisions have been commenced in England but not in Wales. This means that it is very difficult, even for professionals, to discern the substance of planning law in Wales. This leads to increased costs to individuals, communities and businesses, as well as to local planning authorities.

2.21 The planning system in England and Wales relies on the preparation of local development plans, with which individual planning applications should comply. The Planning (Wales) Bill, due to be introduced into the National Assembly for Wales in 2014, will reform plan-making functions in Wales. However, it will not fundamentally address the distinct process of development management and consideration of planning applications, nor the relationship between development management and local development plans.

2.22 The problems with Welsh planning law cannot be dealt with by a technical consolidation alone. This project will therefore consider the merits of a simplified and modernised planning system that is suitable for the needs of Wales, a smaller country with different types of land use, and with a close connection between government bodies. The primary focus of the project will be the reform of the process of development control in Wales. It will also address the relationship between plan-making and development control. A simplified and modernised planning system for Wales will have the potential to promote economic growth, housing supply and protection of the environment, as well as increasing efficiency and reducing transaction costs.

PROTECTING CONSUMER PREPAYMENTS ON RETAILER INSOLVENCY

Autumn 2014 – spring 2016

2.23 Consumers often pay for goods in advance. This may be to budget for big spends, such as at Christmas, or as a deposit for major purchases like cars or new kitchens. On a smaller scale, gift vouchers are a popular purchase. However, recent high-profile retailer insolvencies have highlighted how little protection the consumer has when they have made a prepayment. In 2006, the collapse of Farepak Christmas savings club left many consumers out of pocket and prompted the Office of Fair Trading to conduct a review. More recently, the collapse of Comet reportedly caused consumers to lose £4.7 million in unused gift vouchers.

2.24 When a retailer becomes insolvent, consumers are low down the insolvency priority order. As a consequence, whatever may be available to pay creditors goes to those ranked above them and there is usually little or nothing left over.

2.25 This lack of protection is causing concern. The issues are complex and go to the heart of the insolvency regime. In 1982, the Cork Report rejected greater protection for consumers, noting that consumers typically lose small and affordable amounts, while the effect of an insolvency on suppliers can be catastrophic. However, there are good reasons for giving consumers more protection, not least to maintain consumer confidence in these products. Yet any greater protection for consumers will necessarily lead to less protection for others.

2.26 The Department for Business, Innovation and Skills has asked the Commission to review this area of law. We will undertake an initial study to consider possible ways forward, gathering empirical evidence about the scale of the problem and consulting on possible solutions. The project will not be conducted jointly with the Scottish Law Commission, but we will work with them to consider possible differences in approach to the issue in Scots law and the law of England and Wales.

SENTENCING PROCEDURE

Summer 2014 – summer 2017

2.27 The law on sentencing procedure is contained in a myriad of statutes. Every year, new legislation is enacted either to amend the existing statutes or to create new aspects of sentencing procedure to complement them. The provisions of the new statutes are brought into force at different times by different statutory instruments, and have a variety of transitional arrangements. This makes it difficult, if not impossible at times, for practitioners and the courts to appreciate what the present law of sentencing procedure actually is.

2.28 The courts have repeatedly complained about the complexity of modern sentencing procedure and the difficulties they have navigating through it. There is strong evidence, both from a study of decided cases and from sentencing experts, that many unlawful sentences are being handed down because sentencing tribunals have been unable to find their way through the relevant provisions. This undermines public confidence in sentencing and costs a great deal of public money to rectify on appeal.

2.29 This project will aim to introduce a single sentencing statute that will, thereafter, be the first and only port of call for sentencing tribunals. It will set out the relevant provisions in a clear and logical way. Just as importantly, any changes to sentencing procedure that Parliament wishes to make will be made to that Act and to no other. This will ensure that there is no need for judges and practitioners to look anywhere else. It is not the aim of this project to interfere with mandatory minimum sentences or with sentencing tariffs in general. Those will remain entirely untouched, but the process by which they come to be imposed will be streamlined and much improved.

WILLS

Early 2015 – early 2018

2.30 Although nearly a quarter of a million grants of representation[6] were issued in 2012, it is estimated that 40% or more of the adult population does not have a will. Where there is no will the intestacy rules will apply, but they are a blunt instrument that cannot replace the expression of a person's own wishes. Certain individuals and bodies cannot benefit under the rules, including cohabitants and charities. It is therefore important that people make wills and that the law supports this.

2.31 The primary wills statute, the Wills Act 1837, dates from the Victorian era. The law governing testamentary capacity, the mental capacity to make a will, derives from the 1870 case of *Banks v Goodfellow*.[7] There is concern that the current law discourages some people from making wills, that it is out of step with social and medical developments, and that it may not work in such a way as to give best effect to a person's intentions on death. It has been criticised for being difficult to understand and apply, and for sometimes being unworkable in practice. In the case of mental capacity, this presents a growing problem, since conditions that affect capacity are becoming more common as people live longer.

2.32 This project will review the law of wills, focusing on four key areas that have been identified as potentially needing reform: testamentary capacity, the formalities for a valid will, the rectification of wills, and mutual wills. It will consider whether the law could be reformed to encourage and facilitate will-making in the 21st century: for example, whether it should be updated to take account of developments in technology and medicine. It will also aim to reduce the likelihood of wills being challenged after death, and the incidence of litigation. Such litigation is expensive, can divide families and is a cause of great stress for the bereaved.

[6] A grant of representation provides the court's authority for a representative to deal with the estate of a deceased person.

[7] (1870) LR 5 QB 549

PART 3
FURTHER POTENTIAL PROJECTS

INTRODUCTION

3.1 In this section, we outline a number of proposals that the Law Commission has not been able to take forward as part of the Twelfth Programme, and explain why this is the case. We believe that these proposals could have significant merit as law reform projects. If resources allow, it may prove possible to accept one or more of these projects as references from Ministers during the course of the Twelfth Programme.

CORPORATE CRIMINAL LIABILITY

3.2 The attribution of most forms of corporate criminal liability is still a matter for the common law. In some cases, the requirements of liability are unclear. There have been calls for the reform of corporate criminal liability in order to codify the rules for attributing criminal liability to a corporation. There have also been proposals to replace the current "identification doctrine" with a form of direct corporate liability, and to introduce liability for the collective criminal activities of a corporation's officers and agents.

3.3 Reform in this area would provide a clearer and more robust framework for the prosecution of corporations and their employees and agents who are responsible for criminal wrongs. The Law Commission has a history of looking at issues around corporate liability. In 2010, the Commission prepared some background work for a further project of this type.[8]

3.4 There is widespread support for reform in this area of the law, and a Law Commission project would be topical and timely. A range of consultees, including lawyers, academics and stakeholders from the commercial world, suggested that we undertake such a project. We have also had supportive discussions with a number of interested Government departments.

3.5 However, the relevant issues are not merely legal. There are underlying questions of public policy which may have considerable commercial and social impact. It is important therefore that Government is clear about the parameters within which an independent review should and could operate. These are not simple matters, and unfortunately it proved impossible to afford the issues due consideration in time for the project to be included in the Twelfth Programme.

CRIMINAL LAW IN THE DIGITAL AGE

3.6 In the last decade, the popularity of social networking sites has increased exponentially, creating new challenges for the criminal law. There has been a steady stream of cases in which the use of a social networking site has been at the heart of alleged criminal conduct, whether it be tweeting offensive messages or posting abusive comments on Facebook. However, some forms of online abuse do not easily fall within the compass of any existing criminal offence.

[8] Criminal Liability in Regulatory Contexts (2010) Law Commission Consultation Paper No 195

3.7 One of those forms relates to what the media has called "revenge porn", where a person posts a compromising photograph of a former partner online. In some cases, the victim of this form of activity has committed suicide upon learning what their former partner has done. Yet, if the photograph was taken with the victim's consent, any possible prosecution would be under offences that were not designed to tackle such conduct.

3.8 Clarity in this area of the law is vital, and the need for a review is likely to become more pressing as ways of interacting online develop. The Law Commission is well placed to conduct a scoping study considering criminal law in the digital age. A project in this area was proposed to us by academics and supported by lawyers with the Crown Prosecution Service, as well as other interested parties across Government.

3.9 Ministerial support in accordance with the Protocol was not forthcoming in time for this project to be included in the Twelfth Programme. However, we intend to monitor developments and to keep in touch with officials and others who work in this area.

HIDDEN FEES IN RETIREMENT LEASES

3.10 Concerns have been raised about the fairness of certain lease covenants employed in, and apparently unique to, the retirement leasehold sector. These require the payment of transfer (or "exit") fees, often amounting to thousands of pounds. The payments are triggered by specified events including assignment of the lease, or upon sale of the property in the event of the death or entry into care of the leaseholder.

3.11 In February 2013, the Office of Fair Trading (OFT) completed its investigation into the fairness of these obligations under the Unfair Terms in Consumer Contracts Regulations 1999. The OFT concluded that a number of features made retirement leasehold exit fees potentially unfair. This problem is made worse by a lack of transparency, especially in sales material. The OFT recommended that legislative reform be considered. It explained that typical transfer fees varied between 0.25% and 12.5% of the sale price or open market value of the property concerned. These terms apply at all times during the term of the lease, meaning that the obligation to pay may be triggered multiple times.

3.12 The issues raised in relation to retirement leasehold properties are important in terms of both their financial value and their impact on vulnerable people, such as the elderly and the bereaved. A future project would require an examination of ongoing concerns regarding exit fees, and a review of both leasehold and unfair terms law with a view to recommending appropriate solutions. Although Commissioners considered that there was a strong case for the inclusion of this project in the programme, they reluctantly concluded that there are currently insufficient resources to include this project. It would, however, be suitable for future ministerial referral.

PUBLIC RIGHTS OF WAY AND PERMISSIVE PATHS

3.13 The current legislation on public rights of way is confusing. A number of different types of rights of way have arisen over time, and these rights are now scattered over numerous pieces of legislation which have been much amended. New types of rights of way have been grafted onto a scheme which was constructed around historical rights at common law, some of which are less relevant today or no longer exist at all.

3.14 A number of consultees proposed that the Law Commission should undertake a project to reform and update the law relating to certain, largely non-vehicular, public rights of way, clarifying the nature and extent of those rights. The project would also have considered whether "permissive paths", which are made available to the public by landowners, should enjoy statutory recognition.

3.15 The Department for Environment, Food and Rural Affairs agreed that the legislation could benefit from a review, and the project was also supported in principle by the Department for Transport. However, Government is currently amending the legislation through the Deregulation Bill, and has also recently committed to set up a stakeholder working group on motor vehicle use of unsealed routes. It was considered that a Law Commission project should await the results of both these processes. In the light of these developments, and the merits of competing projects, Commissioners concluded that this project should not feature in the Twelfth Programme. It may, however, be appropriate for a future ministerial reference.

TRUST LAW ARBITRATION

3.16 Arbitration is a method of settling legal disputes privately, without going to court. It is perceived to have advantages over litigation, including the parties' ability to choose the arbitrator (allowing them to select an expert in the relevant area), cost and time savings, and confidentiality. While some trust disputes may be suitable for arbitration, it seems that at present those who create trusts cannot require trustees and beneficiaries to use arbitration, rather than litigation, to resolve their differences. Furthermore, although two or more people of full capacity can enter into a valid stand-alone arbitration agreement to settle a trust dispute, any award will not bind other interested parties.

3.17 The Trust Law Committee and the Chancery Bar Association proposed that the Law Commission should conduct a project to consider the use of arbitration for trust disputes, building on the Trust Law Committee's own work in this area. The project would explore how far arbitration is appropriate for trusts, including private trusts, pension trusts and charitable trusts, and examine how the Arbitration Act 1996 could be amended to facilitate the arbitration of trust disputes. The proposed project was supported by the Department for Business, Innovation and Skills and by the Ministry of Justice.

3.18 A project on trust law arbitration is suitable for the Law Commission and has the potential to offer a range of benefits to all those who set up, benefit from, administer and advise on trusts. Facilitating trust law arbitration could attract trust business to England and Wales and combat competition from other jurisdictions. Commissioners concluded, however, that other projects competing for the Commission's core funding should be given higher priority than work on trust law arbitration, primarily on the basis that they are likely to benefit more people and to target more vulnerable groups within society.

(Signed) DAVID LLOYD JONES, Chairman
ELIZABETH COOKE
DAVID HERTZELL
DAVID ORMEROD
NICHOLAS PAINES

ELAINE LORIMER, Chief Executive
8 July 2014

APPENDIX A
LAW COMMISSION SUGGESTIONS

The Commission suggested that the following areas of law were potentially in need of reform:

(1) Bills of sale

(2) Corporate criminal liability

(3) Fraud by victims of personal injury

(4) Land registration

(5) Selected issues in leasehold law

(6) Sentencing procedure

(7) Social media and the criminal law

(8) Welsh planning law

APPENDIX B
LIST OF CONSULTEES

Proposals were received from the following:

Julia Abrey

Richard Acock

Ageas Insurance Ltd

Nik Antoniades

Grant Morley Argent

Argyle Street Housing Co-operative Ltd

Professor TT Arvind, Newcastle University

Greg Ashby

asra Housing Group

Association of British Insurers

The Association of Corporate Trustees

Association of Personal Injury Lawyers

Ath Gray Housing Co-operative Ltd

District Judge Backhouse

Kay Balaam

The Bar Council

Rupert Barnes

Ron Bartholomew

David Barton

Bedfont Stoney Wall Housing Co-operative Ltd

Belgrave Neighbourhood Co-operative Housing Association Ltd

Nicholas Bevan

Bond Dickinson LLP

Alistair Bould, Pinsent Masons

David Bowles, RSPCA

John Bradfield, Alice Barker Trust

Professor Susan Bright, University of Oxford

British Association for Adoption and Fostering

British Shooting Sports Council

British Transport Police

David Brydon

Keith Bush QC, Legal Wales Foundation

Professor Dermot Cahill, Bangor University

Cathedral Mansions Housing Co-operative Ltd

Chancery Bar Association

Chippenham Housing Co-operative Ltd

Julian Cohen

Confederation of British Industry

Confederation of Co-operative Housing

Keith Conway, Property Litigation Association

Co-op Homes (South) Ltd

Rob Cooper

Dr Simon Cooper, Oxford Brookes University

Co-operative Housing in Partnership

Cossington Housing Co-operative Ltd

Nick Cotton

Council of Her Majesty's Circuit Judges

Council of Mortgage Lenders

Frank Cranmer

Criminal Bar Association

Cross Lances Housing Co-operative Ltd

Crown Prosecution Service

DAC Beachcroft LLP

Dawley Housing Co-operative Ltd

Professor Ian Dennis, University College London

Department for Business, Innovation and Skills

Department for Education

Michael Devaney

Timothy Dutton QC, Association of Regulatory and Disciplinary Lawyers

DWF LLP

Laurence Eastham

Mr Justice Eder

Alex Elphinston

esure Group plc

Lorraine Etherington

Philip Evans

District Judge Exton

Family Justice Council

Forum of Insurance Lawyers

Dr Sara Fovargue, Lancaster University

Henry Frydenson, Association of Contentious Trust and Probate Specialists

Dr Nikki Godden, Newcastle University

Amy Goymour, University of Cambridge

Grand Union Housing Co-operative Ltd

Michael Hall

Emma Hatfield, University of Huddersfield

Rosemary Herbert

District Judge Hickman

Hirst Housing Co-operative Ltd

Professor Nicholas Hopkins, University of Reading

Yvonne Hopkins

Michael Hulme

Dr Catrin Fflur Huws, Centre of Welsh Legal Affairs, Aberystwyth University

Institute of Chartered Accountants in England and Wales

International Underwriting Association of London

Christopher Jessel

Susan Jones

District Judge Jordan

Judges of Birmingham Crown Court

Anne Louise Just

Angela Kennedy

Keoghs LLP

Alistair Kinley, Berrymans Lace Mawer LLP

The Law Society

Stephen Lawson

Legal Ombudsman

Lord Justice Leveson, Sentencing Council

Victor Levy

Mr Justice Lewis

Anna Lindsay-Thinn

Gillian Linford

Nick Lloyd, Nabarro LLP

Local Government Association

David Lunn

Nicholas Macklam

Sir David Maddison

Neil McDougall

Maxine McGill

Metropolitan Police Directorate of Forensic Services

Middlesex Housing Co-operative Ltd

Mind

Ministry of Justice

John Moloney

Christopher Morcom QC

Mosac

Dr Fred Mpala

Simon Mumford

Chief Constable Sir Jon Murphy, National Police Lead for the Crime Business Area

Charles Mynors

Hetti Nanton

National Ballistics Intelligence Service

Professor Sarah Nield, University of Southampton

Old Isleworth Housing Co-operative Ltd

Patricia O'Neil

District Judge Parker

Professor Michael Parker Pearson, University College London

Jay Parmar, British Vehicle Renting and Leasing Association

Chris Pashley

Liz Peace CBE, British Property Federation

Peel Street Housing Co-operative Ltd

Personal Injuries Bar Association

Dr Martin Petrin, University College London

Ann Phillips, Charity Law Association

Gerard Pitt

QBE Insurance Group Ltd

Malcolm Ramsay

Colin Ray, Intrusive Footpaths Campaign

Master Richard Roberts

Ross Walk Housing Co-operative Ltd

RSA Insurance Group plc

Russell-Cooke LLP

Peter Sanguinetti

Caroline Sawyer

Senacre Housing Co-operative Ltd

Seymour Housing Co-operative Ltd

Mark Shelton

Nick Shepherd

Paula-Jane Shepherd

Mr Justice Silber

Richard Smithies

Professor John Spencer QC, University of Cambridge

Gill Steel

Clayton Stockwell

Michael Swainston QC

Robin Tam QC

Rod Thomas

Thompsons Solicitors

Thornholme Housing Co-operative Ltd

Transportation Claims Ltd

Trust Law Committee

Lord Justice Underhill

Lord Justice Vos

Water Tower Housing Co-operative Ltd

Professor Thomas Glyn Watkin

Waverley (Eighth) Co-operative Housing Association Ltd

Richard Webber

Weightmans LLP

Arthur Weir, City of Westminster and Holborn Law Society

Wellington Housing Co-operative Ltd

Welsh Government

Angela Williams, Citizens Advice Cymru

Charlotte Williams

Teresa Williams

Debbie Wiseman

Wrigleys Solicitors LLP

Professor Helen Xanthaki, IALS Think Tank on Law Reform

Dr Lu Xu, University of East Anglia

Peter Yardley